Knit Dishcl

15 **Extremely Easy** Designs Inspired by Quilt Blocks!

MAKING DISHCLOTHS IS QUICK AND FUN!
EVEN BETTER, THIS PLENTIFUL COLLECTION OF
15 DESIGNS CAN BE KNITTED—OR KNOOKED!

The Knook® is an exciting new tool, a special crochet hook that replaces knitting needles. It creates true knitted fabric while the ttached cord prevents dropped stitches. Knook kits are available at 'our local craft store. You can also get them from LeisureArts.com, vhere you'll find excellent videos and free patterns for the Knook. In this book, we've included instructions both for knitting and knooking the patchwork-inspired dishcloths. For a very special gift that will always be cherished, sew together multiples of each design, fashioning a cozy "quilt" afghan.

Meet Julie A. Ray

"I really enjoy the quickness of making dishcloths," says Julie Ray. "I wanted to bring my love of quilting into my love of knitting, thus, quilt block dishcloths!" Julie not only knits, she also crochets, sews, and does cross stitch, fitting lots of creativity into her busy days.

Julie says, "My wonderful husband Richard is a chef. I have three children, two stepchildren, a daughter-in-law, and three grandkids, and I enjoy visiting with my dad, Darrel Smith. My creativity comes from my mom, Shirley Smith, who passed away last year. She encouraged me in all that I did, including designing my own patterns."

"So now I encourage everyone to give knitting dishcloths a try—they're beginner-friendly, and they open a door to all kinds of projects. The possibilities are endless, and so is the joy of creating something for someone you love."

Contents

LEISURE ARTS, INC.
Maumelle, Arkansas

AMISH DIAMOND

BEGINNER

Shown on Front Cover.

FINISHED SIZE:
7 1/2"w x 9 1/2"h (19 cm x 24 cm)

MATERIALS
Medium Weight Cotton Yarn (MEDIUM 4)
[2.5 ounces, 120 yards (71 grams, 109 meters) per ball]: One ball
Needles: Straight knitting needles, size 8 (5 mm) **or** size needed for gauge
Knook: Size H (5 mm) **or** size needed for gauge

GAUGE:
In Stockinette Stitch (knit one row, purl one row), 9 sts and 13 rows = 2" (5 cm)

The **dishcloth** may be made by following the written instructions or by following the chart for Rows 9-55 (see *Charts, page 23*). Only **odd numbered** rows are charted. Refer to Row 8 for all **even numbered** rows.

Dishcloth

Needles: Cast on 34 sts.

Knook: Ch 34; pick up 33 sts on foundation ch: 34 sts.

Rows 1-7: Knit across.

Row 8 AND ALL WRONG SIDE ROWS THROUGH Row 56: K5, P 24, K5.

Row 9 (Right side)**:** K 11, P 12, K 11.

Row 11: K 11, P 12, K 11.

Row 13: K 11, P 12, K 11.

Row 15: K 11, P 12, K 11.

Row 17: K 11, P 12, K 11.

Row 19: K 11, P 12, K 11.

Row 21: K5, P6, K 12, P6, K5.

Row 23: K5, P6, K5, P2, K5, P6, K5.

Row 25: K5, P6, K4, P4, K4, P6, K5.

Row 27: K5, P6, (K3, P6) twice, K5.

Row 29: K5, P6, K2, P8, K2, P6, K5.

Row 31: K5, P6, K1, P 10, K1, P6, K5.

Row 33: K5, P6, K1, P 10, K1, P6, K5.

Row 35: K5, P6, K2, P8, K2, K5.

Row 37: K5, P6, (K3, P6) twic K5.

Row 39: K5, P6, K4, P4, K4, K5.

Row 41: K5, P6, K5, P2, K5, K5.

Row 43: K5, P6, K 12, P6, K5

Row 45: K 11, P 12, K 11.

Row 47: K 11, P 12, K 11.

Row 49: K 11, P 12, K 11.

Row 51: K 11, P 12, K 11.

Row 53: K 11, P 12, K 11.

Row 55: K 11, P 12, K 11.

Rows 57-63: Knit across.

Bind off all sts in **knit**.

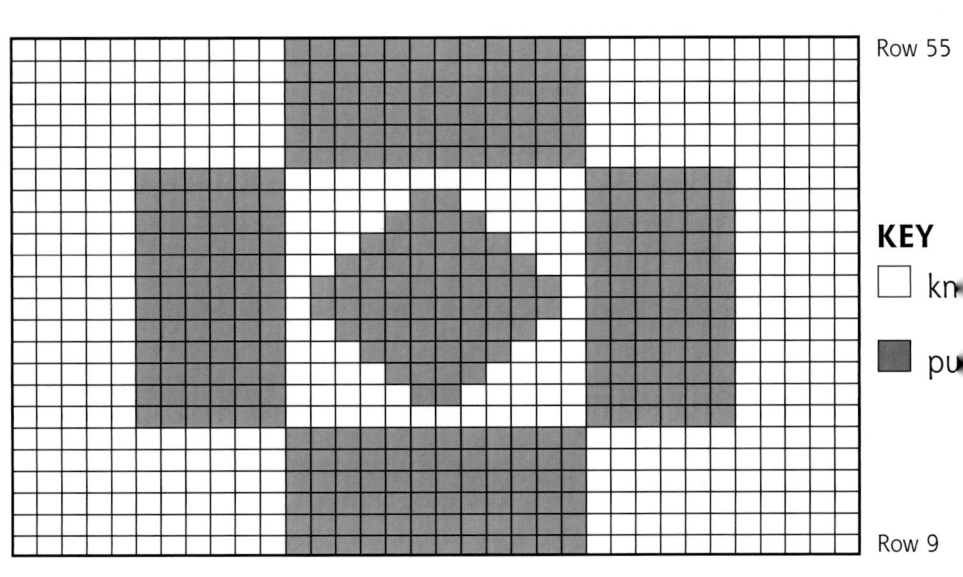

'ARIABLE STAR

ɔwn on *Front Cover.*

ɴISHED SIZE:
'2"w x 9½"h (19 cm x 24 cm)

ATERIALS
ɜdium Weight
tton Yarn
[2.5 ounces, 120 yards
(71 grams, 109 meters) per
ball]: One ball
ɜedles: Straight knitting
needles, size 8 (5 mm) **or**
size needed for gauge
ɪook: Size H (5 mm) **or**
size needed for gauge

ɪUGE:
Stockinette Stitch
ɪit one row, purl one row),
ɜts and 13 rows = 2" (5 cm)

ɪe **dishcloth** may be made
y following the written
ɪstructions or by following
ɪe chart for Rows 9-55
ee *Charts, page 23*). Only
dd numbered rows are
ɪarted. Refer to Row 8 for
ɪl **even numbered** rows.

ishcloth

ɜedles: Cast on 34 sts.

ɪook: Ch 34; pick up 33 sts on
undation ch: 34 sts.

ɔws 1-7: Knit across.

ɔw 8 AND ALL WRONG SIDE ƆWS THROUGH Row 56: K5, 24, K5.

w 9 (Right side)**:** K 11, P1, 10, P1, K 11.

Row 11: K 11, P2, K8, P2, K 11.

Row 13: K 11, P3, K6, P3, K 11.

Row 15: K 11, P4, K4, P4, K 11.

Row 17: K 11, P5, K2, P5, K 11.

Row 19: K 11, P 12, K 11.

Row 21: K5, P6, K5, P2, K5, P6, K5.

Row 23: K6, P5, K4, P4, K4, P5, K6.

Row 25: K7, P4, K3, P6, K3, P4, K7.

Row 27: K8, P3, K2, P8, K2, P3, K8.

Row 29: K9, P2, K1, P 10, K1, P2, K9.

Row 31: K 10, P 14, K 10.

Row 33: K 10, P 14, K 10.

Row 35: K9, P2, K1, P 10, K1, P2, K9.

Row 37: K8, P3, K2, P8, K2, P3, K8.

Row 39: K7, P4, K3, P6, K3, P4, K7.

Row 41: K6, P5, K4, P4, K4, P5, K6.

Row 43: K5, P6, K5, P2, K5, P6, K5.

Row 45: K 11, P 12, K 11.

Row 47: K 11, P5, K2, P5, K 11.

Row 49: K 11, P4, K4, P4, K 11.

Row 51: K 11, P3, K6, P3, K 11.

Row 53: K 11, P2, K8, P2, K 11.

Row 55: K 11, P1, K 10, P1, K 11.

Rows 57-63: Knit across.

Bind off all sts in **knit**.

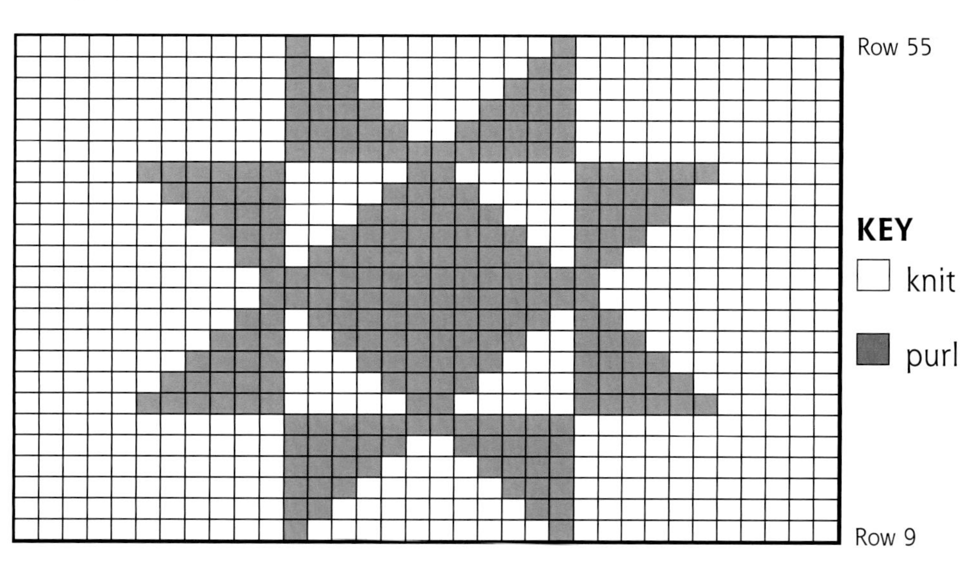

Make this
thurs @ 2:00
sign-up here
Sondra
CHRISTY
Jane
Patti

PINWHEEL 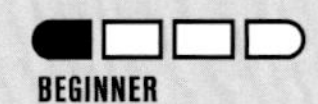

Shown on Front Cover.

FINISHED SIZE:
7½"w x 9½"h (19 cm x 24 cm)

MATERIALS
Medium Weight Cotton Yarn (MEDIUM 4)
[2.5 ounces, 120 yards (71 grams, 109 meters) per ball]: One ball
Needles: Straight knitting needles, size 8 (5 mm) **or** size needed for gauge
Knook: Size H (5 mm) **or** size needed for gauge

GAUGE:
In Stockinette Stitch (knit one row, purl one row), 9 sts and 13 rows = 2" (5 cm)

The **dishcloth** may be made by following the written instructions or by following the chart for Rows 9-55 (*see Charts, page 23*). Only **odd numbered** rows are charted. Refer to Row 8 for all **even numbered** rows.

Dishcloth

Needles: Cast on 34 sts.

Knook: Ch 34; pick up 33 sts on foundation ch: 34 sts.

Rows 1-7: Knit across.

Row 8 AND ALL WRONG SIDE ROWS THROUGH Row 56: K5, P 24, K5.

Row 9 (Right side)**:** K5, P6, K5, P7, K5, P1, K5.

Row 11: K6, P5, K4, P2, K1, P5, K4, P2, K5.

Row 13: K7, P4, K3, P3, K2, P4, K3, P3, K5.

Row 15: K8, P3, K2, P4, K3, P3, K2, P4, K5.

Row 17: K9, P2, K1, P5, K4, P2, K1, P5, K5.

Row 19: K 10, (P7, K5) twice.

Row 21: (K5, P7) twice, K 10.

Row 23: K5, P5, K1, P2, K4, P5, K1, P2, K9.

Row 25: K5, P4, K2, P3, K3, P4, K2, P3, K8.

Row 27: K5, P3, K3, P4, K2, P3, K3, P4, K7.

Row 29: K5, P2, K4, P5, K1, P2, K4, P5, K6.

Row 31: K5, P1, K5, P7, K5, P6, K5.

Row 33: Repeat Row 9.

Row 35: Repeat Row 11.

Row 37: Repeat Row 13.

Row 39: Repeat Row 15.

Row 41: Repeat Row 17.

Row 43: K 10, (P7, K5) twice.

Row 45: (K5, P7) twice, K 10.

Row 47: Repeat Row 23.

Row 49: Repeat Row 25.

Row 51: Repeat Row 27.

Row 53: Repeat Row 29.

Row 55: Repeat Row 31.

Rows 57-63: Knit across.

Bind off all sts in **knit**.

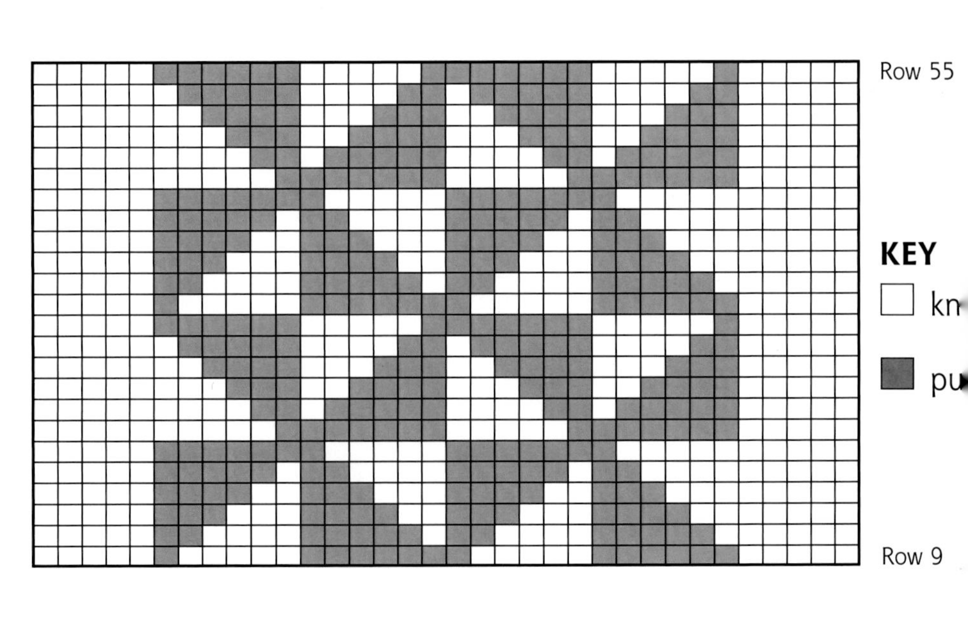

ARROW POINT

BEGINNER

own on page 4.

NISHED SIZE:
/2"w x 9 1/2"h (19 cm x 24 cm)

ATERIALS
edium Weight
tton Yarn
MEDIUM 4
[2.5 ounces, 120 yards
(71 grams, 109 meters) per
ball]: One ball
eedles: Straight knitting
needles, size 8 (5 mm) **or**
size needed for gauge
ook: Size H (5 mm) **or**
size needed for gauge

AUGE:
Stockinette Stitch
nit one row, purl one row),
sts and 13 rows = 2" (5 cm)

he **dishcloth** may be made
y following the written
nstructions or by following
he chart for Rows 9-55
see *Charts, page 23*). Only
dd numbered rows are
harted. Refer to Row 8 for
ll **even numbered** rows.

ishcloth

eedles: Cast on 34 sts.

ook: Ch 34; pick up 33 sts on
undation ch: 34 sts.

ows 1-7: Knit across.

ow 8 AND ALL WRONG SIDE OWS THROUGH Row 56: K5,
24, K5.

ow 9 (Right side)**:** K6, P5, K1,
10, K1, P5, K6.

Row 11: K7, P4, K2, P8, K2, P4, K7.

Row 13: K8, P3, K3, P6, K3, P3, K8.

Row 15: K9, P2, K4, P4, K4, P2, K9.

Row 17: K 10, P1, K5, P2, K5, P1, K 10.

Row 19: Knit across.

Row 21: K6, P5, K 12, P5, K6.

Row 23: K7, P5, K 10, P5, K7.

Row 25: K8, (P5, K8) twice.

Row 27: K9, P5, K6, P5, K9.

Row 29: K 10, P5, K4, P5, K 10.

Row 31: K 11, P5, K2, P5, K 11.

Row 33: K 11, P5, K2, P5, K 11.

Row 35: K 10, P5, K4, P5, K 10.

Row 37: K9, P5, K6, P5, K9.

Row 39: K8, (P5, K8) twice.

Row 41: K7, P5, K 10, P5, K7.

Row 43: K6, P5, K 12, P5, K6.

Row 45: Knit across.

Row 47: K 10, P1, K5, P2, K5, P1, K 10.

Row 49: K9, P2, K4, P4, K4, P2, K9.

Row 51: K8, P3, K3, P6, K3, P3, K8.

Row 53: K7, P4, K2, P8, K2, P4, K7.

Row 55: K6, P5, K1, P 10, K1, P5, K6.

Rows 57-63: Knit across.

Bind off all sts in **knit**.

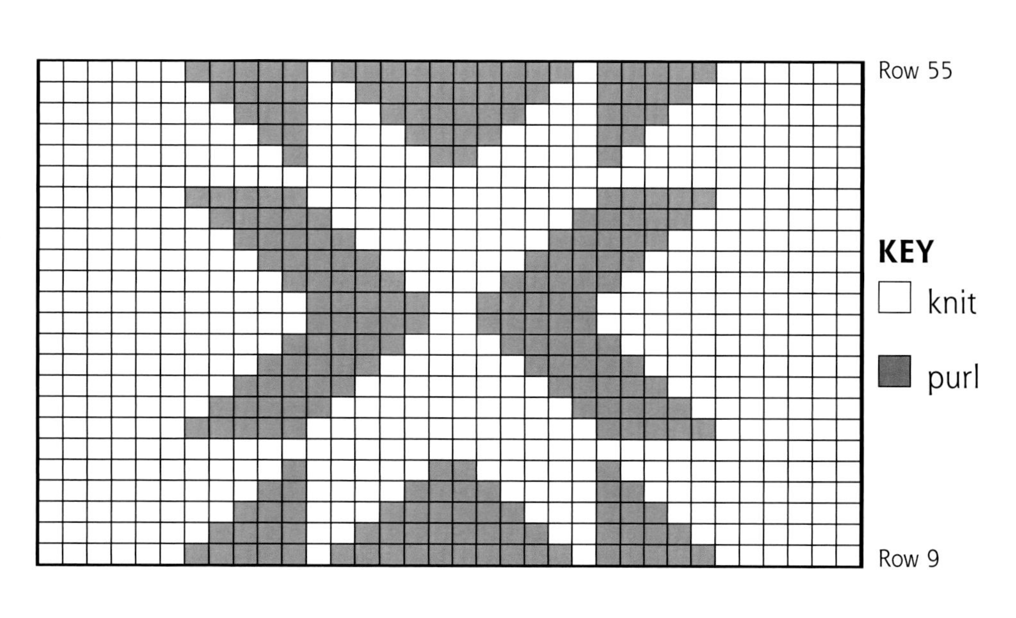

KING'S CROWN

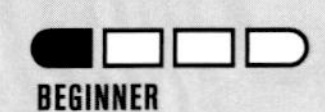

Shown on page 4.

FINISHED SIZE:
7 1/2"w x 9 1/2"h (19 cm x 24 cm)

MATERIALS
Medium Weight Cotton Yarn (MEDIUM 4)
[2.5 ounces, 120 yards (71 grams, 109 meters) per ball]: One ball
Needles: Straight knitting needles, size 8 (5 mm) **or** size needed for gauge
Knook: Size H (5 mm) **or** size needed for gauge

GAUGE:
In Stockinette Stitch (knit one row, purl one row), 9 sts and 13 rows = 2" (5 cm)

The **dishcloth** may be made by following the written instructions or by following the chart for Rows 9-55 (see *Charts, page 23*). Only **odd numbered** rows are charted. Refer to Row 8 for all **even numbered** rows.

Dishcloth

Needles: Cast on 34 sts.

Knook: Ch 34; pick up 33 sts on foundation ch: 34 sts.

Rows 1-7: Knit across.

Row 8 AND ALL WRONG SIDE ROWS THROUGH Row 56: K5, P 24, K5.

Row 9 (Right side)**:** K 11, P5, K2, P5, K 11.

Row 11: K 11, P4, K4, P4, K 11.

Row 13: K 11, P3, K6, P3, K 11.

Row 15: K 11, P2, K8, P2, K 11.

Row 17: K 11, P1, K 10, P1, K 11.

Row 19: Knit across.

Row 21: K5, P5, K1, P 12, K1, P5, K5.

Row 23: K5, P4, K2, P 12, K2, P4, K5.

Row 25: K5, P3, K3, P 12, K3, P3, K5.

Row 27: K5, P2, K4, P 12, K4, P2, K5.

Row 29: K5, P1, K5, P 12, K5, P1, K5.

Row 31: K 11, P 12, K 11.

Row 33: K 11, P 12, K 11.

Row 35: K5, P1, K5, P 12, K5 P1, K5.

Row 37: K5 P2, K4, P 12, K4, K5.

Row 39: K5, P3, K3, P 12, K3 P3, K5.

Row 41: K5, P4, K2, P 12, K2 P4, K5.

Row 43: K5, P5, K1, P 12, K1 P5, K5.

Row 45: Knit across.

Row 47: K 11, P1, K 10, P1, K 11.

Row 49: K 11, P2, K8, P2, K

Row 51: K 11, P3, K6, P3, K 1

Row 53: K 11, P4, K4, P4, K 1

Row 55: K 11, P5, K2, P5, K 1

Rows 57-63: Knit across.

Bind off all sts in **knit**.

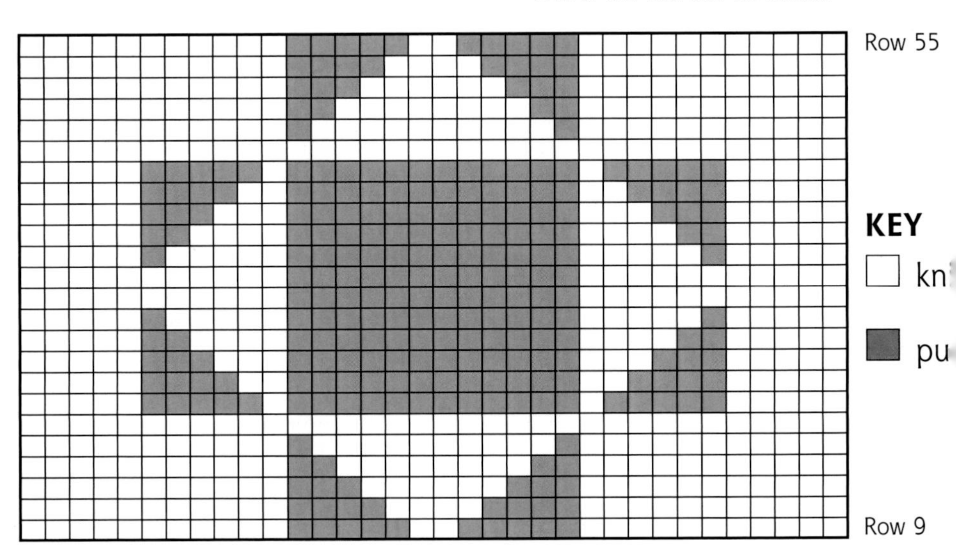

BACHELOR'S PUZZLE

Shown on page 4.

FINISHED SIZE:
7½"w x 9½"h (19 cm x 24 cm)

MATERIALS
Medium Weight Cotton Yarn

[2.5 ounces, 120 yards (71 grams, 109 meters) per ball]: One ball
Needles: Straight knitting needles, size 8 (5 mm) **or** size needed for gauge
Knook: Size H (5 mm) **or** size needed for gauge

GAUGE:
In Stockinette Stitch (knit one row, purl one row), 9 sts and 13 rows = 2" (5 cm)

The **dishcloth** may be made by following the written instructions or by following the chart for Rows 9-55 (see *Charts, page 23*). Only **odd numbered** rows are charted. Refer to Row 8 for all **even numbered** rows.

Dishcloth

Needles: Cast on 34 sts.

Knook: Ch 34; pick up 33 sts on foundation ch: 34 sts.

Rows 1-7: Knit across.

Row 8 AND ALL WRONG SIDE ROWS THROUGH Row 56: K5, P 24, K5.

Row 9 (Right side)**:** K 10, P1, K6, P7, K 10.

Row 11: K9, P2, K6, P8, K9.

Row 13: K8, P3, K6, P9, K8.

Row 15: K7, P4, K6, P 10, K7.

Row 17: K6, P5, K6, P 11, K6.

Row 19: K5, P6, K6, P 12, K5.

Row 21: K5, P 18, K 11.

Row 23: K5, P 11, K2, P5, K 11.

Row 25: K5, P 10, K4, P4, K 11.

Row 27: K5, P9, K6, P3, K 11.

Row 29: K5, P8, K8, P2, K 11.

Row 31: K5, P7, K 10, P1, K 11.

Row 33: K 11, P1, K 10, P7, K5.

Row 35: K 11, P2, K8, P8, K5

Row 37: K 11, P3, K6, P9, K5

Row 39: K 11, P4, K4, P 10, K

Row 41: K 11, P5, K2, P 11, K

Row 43: K 11, P 18, K5.

Row 45: K5, P 12, K6, P6, K5

Row 47: K6, P 11, K6, P5, K6

Row 49: K7, P 10, K6, P4, K7

Row 51: K8, P9, K6, P3, K8.

Row 53: K9, P8, K6, P2, K9.

Row 55: K 10, P7, K6, P1, K 1

Rows 57-63: Knit across.

Bind off all sts in **knit**.

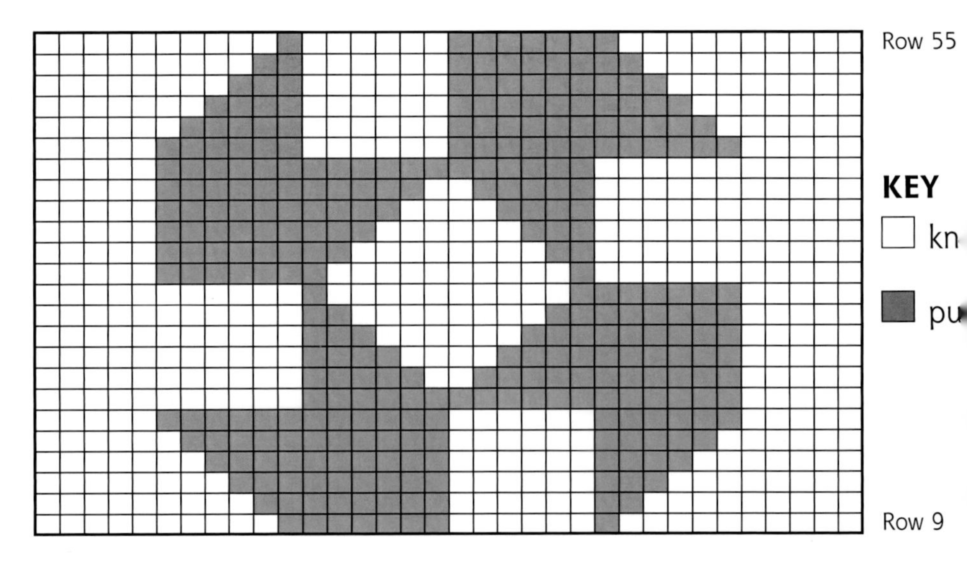

KEY
kn
pu

‍OLD MAID'S PUZZLE

BEGINNER

own on page 9.

NISHED SIZE:
½"w x 9½"h (19 cm x 24 cm)

ATERIALS
edium Weight tton Yarn [1.75 ounces, 80 yards (50 grams, 73 meters) per ball]: One ball

MEDIUM 4

eedles: Straight knitting needles, size 8 (5 mm) **or** size needed for gauge

ook: Size H (5 mm) **or** size needed for gauge

AUGE:
Stockinette Stitch
nit one row, purl one row),
sts and 13 rows = 2" (5 cm)

he **dishcloth** may be made y following the written nstructions or by following he chart for Rows 9-55 see *Charts, page 23*). Only **dd numbered** rows are harted. Refer to Row 8 for ll **even numbered** rows.

ishcloth

eedles: Cast on 34 sts.

ook: Ch 34; pick up 33 sts on undation ch: 34 sts.

ows 1-7: Knit across.

ow 8 AND ALL WRONG SIDE OWS THROUGH Row 56: K5, 24, K5.

ow 9 (Right side)**:** K 10, P1, 6, P1, K5, P1, K 10.

Row 11: K9, P2, K6, P2, K4, P2, K9.

Row 13: K8, P3, K6, P3, K3, P3, K8.

Row 15: K7, P4, K6, P4, K2, P4, K7.

Row 17: (K6, P5) twice, K1, P5, K6.

Row 19: K5, P6, K6, P 12, K5.

Row 21: K 11, P 13, K 10.

Row 23: K 11, P5, K1, P8, K9.

Row 25: K 11, P4, K2, P9, K8.

Row 27: K 11, P3, K3, P 10, K7.

Row 29: K 11, P2, K4, P 11, K6.

Row 31: K 11, P1, K5, P 12, K5.

Row 33: K5, P 12, K5, P1, K 11.

Row 35: K6, P 11, K4, P2, K 11.

Row 37: K7, P 10, K3, P3, K 11.

Row 39: K8, P9, K2, P4, K 11.

Row 41: K9, P8, K1, P5, K 11.

Row 43: K 10, P 13, K 11.

Row 45: K5, P 12, K6, P6, K5.

Row 47: K6, P5, K1, (P5, K6) twice.

Row 49: K7, P4, K2, P4, K6, P4, K7.

Row 51: K8, P3, K3, P3, K6, P3, K8.

Row 53: K9, P2, K4, P2, K6, P2, K9.

Row 55: K 10, P1, K5, P1, K6, P1, K 10.

Rows 57-63: Knit across.

Bind off all sts in **knit**.

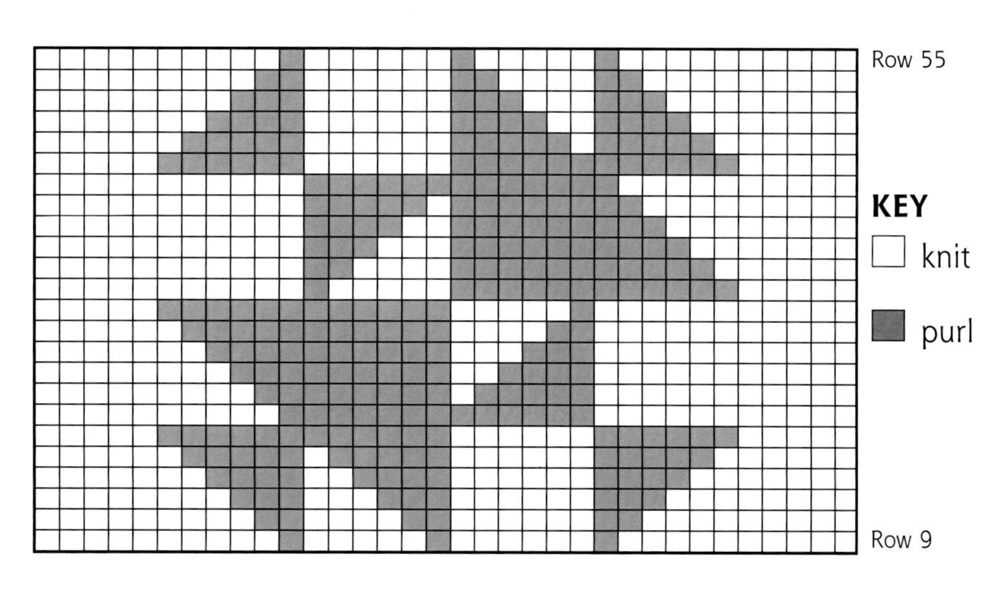

DUTCHMAN'S PUZZLE

Shown on page 9.

FINISHED SIZE:
7¹/₂"w x 9¹/₂"h (19 cm x 24 cm)

MATERIALS
Medium Weight Cotton Yarn

[1.75 ounces, 80 yards (50 grams, 73 meters) per ball]: One ball
Needles: Straight knitting needles, size 8 (5 mm) **or** size needed for gauge
Knook: Size H (5 mm) **or** size needed for gauge

GAUGE:
In Stockinette Stitch (knit one row, purl one row), 9 sts and 13 rows = 2" (5 cm)

The **dishcloth** may be made by following the written instructions or by following the chart for Rows 9-55 (see *Charts, page 23*). Only **odd numbered** rows are charted. Refer to Row 8 for all **even numbered** rows.

Dishcloth

Needles: Cast on 34 sts.

Knook: Ch 34; pick up 33 sts on foundation ch: 34 sts.

Rows 1-7: Knit across.

Row 8 AND ALL WRONG SIDE ROWS THROUGH Row 56: K5, P 24, K5.

Row 9 (Right side)**:** K 10, P2, (K5, P1) twice, K 10.

Row 11: K9, P4, (K4, P2) twice, K9.

Row 13: K8, P6, (K3, P3) twice, K8.

Row 15: K7, P8, (K2, P4) twice, K7.

Row 17: K6, P 10, (K1, P5) twice, K6.

Row 19: K5, P 24, K5.

Row 21: K 10, P2, K5, P 12, K5.

Row 23: K9, P4, K4, P5, K1, P5, K6.

Row 25: K8, P6, K3, P4, K2, P4, K7.

Row 27: K7, P8, K2, P3, K3, P3, K8.

Row 29: K6, P 10, K1, P2, K4, P2, K9.

Row 31: K5, P 13, K5, P1, K 10.

Row 33: K 10, P1, K5, P 13, K5.

Row 35: K9, P2, K4, P2, K1, P 10, K6.

Row 37: K8, P3, K3, P3, K2, P
K7.

Row 39: K7, P4, K2, P4, K3, P
K8.

Row 41: K6, P5, K1, P5, K4, P
K9.

Row 43: K5, P 12, K5, P2, K 1

Row 45: K5, P 24, K5.

Row 47: K6, (P5, K1) twice, P 10, K6.

Row 49: K7, (P4, K2) twice, P8
K7.

Row 51: K8, (P3, K3) twice, P6
K8.

Row 53: K9, (P2, K4) twice, P4
K9.

Row 55: K 10, (P1, K5) twice, P2, K 10.

Rows 57-63: Knit across.

Bind off all sts in **knit**.

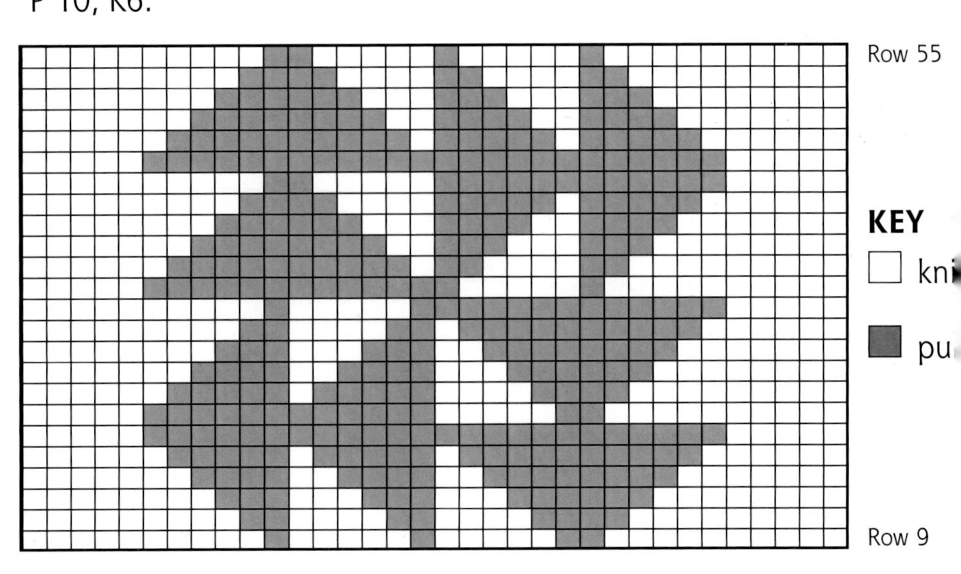

▪INE PATCH

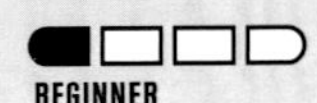

›wn on page 21.

▪ISHED SIZE:
₂"w x 9½"h (19 cm x 24 cm)

▪ATERIALS
▪edium Weight
▪tton Yarn
[2.5 ounces, 120 yards
(71 grams, 109 meters) per
ball]: One ball
▪**eedles:** Straight knitting
needles, size 8 (5 mm) **or**
size needed for gauge
▪**ook:** Size H (5 mm) **or**
size needed for gauge

▪UGE:
Stockinette Stitch
▪nit one row, purl one row),
▪ts and 13 rows = 2" (5 cm)

▪he **dishcloth** may be made
▪y following the written
▪nstructions or by following
▪he chart for Rows 9-55
(see *Charts, page 23*). Only
▪**dd numbered** rows are
▪harted. Refer to Row 8 for
▪ll **even numbered** rows.

▪ishcloth

▪**eedles:** Cast on 34 sts.

▪**ook:** Ch 34; pick up 33 sts on
▪undation ch: 34 sts.

▪**ows 1-7:** Knit across.

▪**ow 8 AND ALL WRONG SIDE
▪OWS THROUGH Row 56:** K5,
▪24, K5.

Row 9 (Right side)**:** K 13, P8, K 13.

Row 11: K 13, P8, K 13.

Row 13: K 13, P8, K 13.

Row 15: K 13, P8, K 13.

Row 17: K 13, P8, K 13.

Row 19: K 13, P8, K 13.

Row 21: K 13, P8, K 13.

Row 23: K 13, P8, K 13.

Row 25: K5, P8, K8, P8, K5.

Row 27: K5, P8, K8, P8, K5.

Row 29: K5, P8, K8, P8, K5.

Row 31: K5, P8, K8, P8, K5.

Row 33: K5, P8, K8, P8, K5.

Row 35: K5, P8, K8, P8, K5.

Row 37: K5, P8, K8, P8, K5.

Row 39: K5, P8, K8, P8, K5.

Row 41: K 13, P8, K 13.

Row 43: K 13, P8, K 13.

Row 45: K 13, P8, K 13.

Row 47: K 13, P8, K 13.

Row 49: K 13, P8, K 13.

Row 51: K 13, P8, K 13.

Row 53: K 13, P8, K 13.

Row 55: K 13, P8, K 13.

Rows 57-63: Knit across.

Bind off all sts in **knit**.

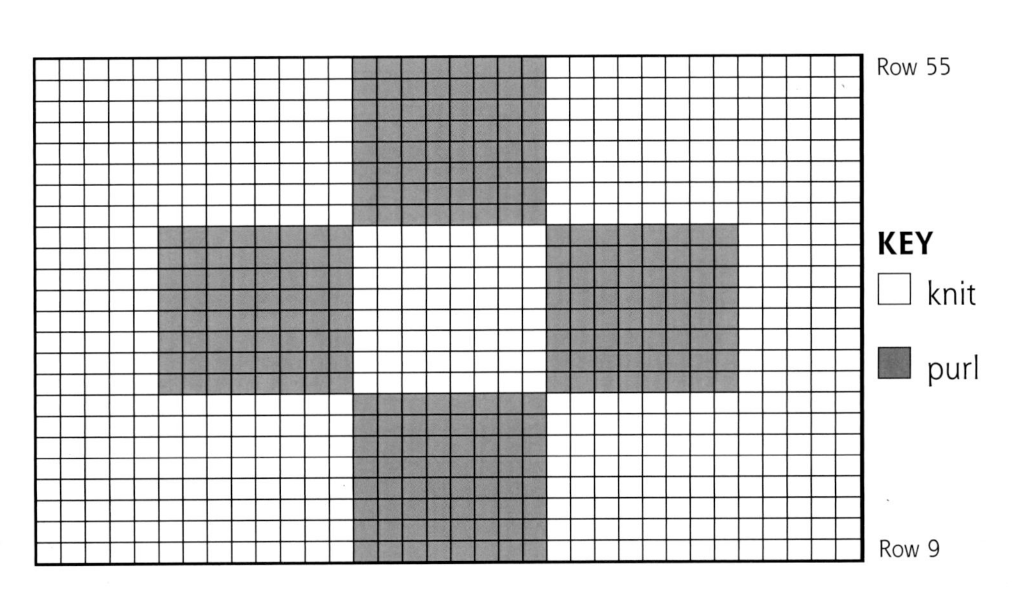

FRIENDSHIP STAR

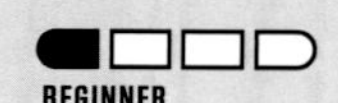

Shown on page 21.

FINISHED SIZE:
7½"w x 9½"h (19 cm x 24 cm)

MATERIALS
Medium Weight Cotton Yarn
[2.5 ounces, 120 yards (71 grams, 109 meters) per ball]: One ball
Needles: Straight knitting needles, size 8 (5 mm) **or** size needed for gauge
Knook: Size H (5 mm) **or** size needed for gauge

GAUGE:
In Stockinette Stitch (knit one row, purl one row), 9 sts and 13 rows = 2" (5 cm)

> The **dishcloth** may be made by following the written instructions or by following the chart for Rows 9-55 (see *Charts, page 23*). Only **odd numbered** rows are charted. Refer to Row 8 for all **even numbered** rows.

Dishcloth

Needles: Cast on 34 sts.

Knook: Ch 34; pick up 33 sts on foundation ch: 34 sts.

Rows 1-7: Knit across.

Row 8 AND ALL WRONG SIDE ROWS THROUGH Row 56: K5, P 24, K5.

Row 9 (Right side)**:** K5, P 15, K1, P8, K5.

Row 11: K5, P 14, K2, P8, K5.

Row 13: K5, P 13, K3, P8, K5.

Row 15: K5, P 12, K4, P8, K5.

Row 17: K5, P 11, K5, P8, K5.

Row 19: K5, P 10, K6, P8, K5.

Row 21: K5, P9, K7, P8, K5.

Row 23: K5, P8, K8, P8, K5.

Row 25: K 13, P8, K1, P7, K5.

Row 27: K5, P1, K7, P8, K2, P6, K5.

Row 29: K5, P2, K6, P8, K3, P5, K5.

Row 31: K5, P3, K5, P8, K4, P4, K5.

Row 33: K5, P4, K4, P8, K5, P3, K5.

Row 35: K5, P5, K3, P8, K6, K5.

Row 37: K5, P6, K2, P8, K7, K5.

Row 39: K5, P7, K1, P8, K 13

Row 41: K5, P8, K8, P8, K5.

Row 43: K5, P8, K7, P9, K5.

Row 45: K5, P8, K6, P 10, K5

Row 47: K5, P8, K5, P 11, K5

Row 49: K5, P8, K4, P 12, K5

Row 51: K5, P8, K3, P 13, K5.

Row 53: K5, P8, K2, P 14, K5.

Row 55: K5, P8, K1, P 15, K5.

Rows 57-63: Knit across.

Bind off all sts in **knit**.

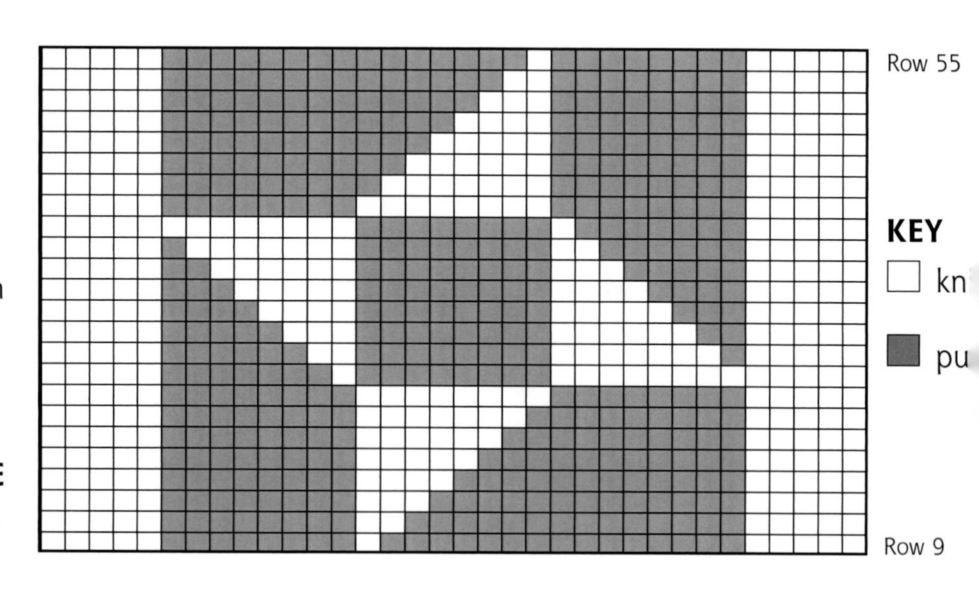

VINDBLOWN SQUARE

BEGINNER

›wn on page 21.

IISHED SIZE:
₂"w x 9½"h (19 cm x 24 cm)

ATERIALS
edium Weight MEDIUM 4
tton Yarn
2.5 ounces, 120 yards
71 grams, 109 meters) per
ball]: One ball
eedles: Straight knitting
needles, size 8 (5 mm) **or**
size needed for gauge
ook: Size H (5 mm) **or**
size needed for gauge

AUGE:
Stockinette Stitch
nit one row, purl one row),
sts and 13 rows = 2" (5 cm)

he **dishcloth** may be made
y following the written
nstructions or by following
he chart for Rows 9-55
ee *Charts, page 23*). Only
dd numbered rows are
harted. Refer to Row 8 for
ll **even numbered** rows.

ishcloth

eedles: Cast on 34 sts.

ook: Ch 34; pick up 33 sts on
undation ch: 34 sts.

ows 1-7: Knit across.

ow 8 AND ALL WRONG SIDE OWS THROUGH Row 56: K5, 24, K5.

ow 9 (Right side)**:** K5, P 13, 10, P1, K5.

Row 11: K6, P 10, K1, P2, K8, P2, K5.

Row 13: K7, P8, K2, P3, K6, P3, K5.

Row 15: K8, P6, K3, P4, K4, P4, K5.

Row 17: K9, P4, K4, P5, K2, P5, K5.

Row 19: K 10, P2, K5, P 12, K5.

Row 21: K 10, P 19, K5.

Row 23: K9, P7, K2, P5, K1, P5, K5.

Row 25: K8, P7, K4, P4, K2, P4, K5.

Row 27: K7, P7, K6, P3, K3, P3, K5.

Row 29: K6, P7, K8, P2, K4, P2, K5.

Row 31: K5, P7, K 10, (P1, K5) twice.

Row 33: (K5, P1) twice, K 10, P7, K5.

Row 35: K5, P2, K4, P2, K8, P7, K6.

Row 37: K5, P3, K3, P3, K6, P7, K7.

Row 39: K5, P4, K2, P4, K4, P7, K8.

Row 41: K5, P5, K1, P5, K2, P7, K9.

Row 43: K5, P 19, K 10.

Row 45: K5, P 12, K5, P2, K 10.

Row 47: K5, P5, K2, P5, K4, P4, K9.

Row 49: K5, P4, K4, P4, K3, P6, K8.

Row 51: K5, P3, K6, P3, K2, P8, K7.

Row 53: K5, P2, K8, P2, K1, P 10, K6.

Row 55: K5, P1, K 10, P 13, K5.

Rows 57-63: Knit across.

Bind off all sts in **knit**.

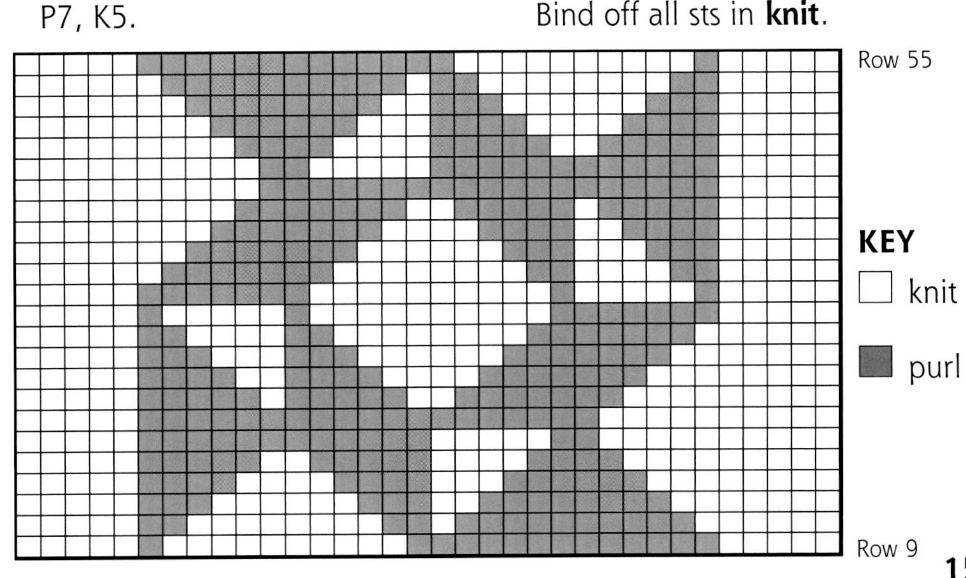

HOUSE

Shown on page 21.

FINISHED SIZE:
$7^1/_2$"w x $9^1/_2$"h (19 cm x 24 cm)

MATERIALS
Medium Weight Cotton Yarn

[2.5 ounces, 120 yards (71 grams, 109 meters) per ball]: One ball
Needles: Straight knitting needles, size 8 (5 mm) **or** size needed for gauge
Knook: Size H (5 mm) **or** size needed for gauge

GAUGE:
In Stockinette Stitch (knit one row, purl one row), 9 sts and 13 rows = 2" (5 cm)

The **dishcloth** may be made by following the written instructions or by following the chart for Rows 9-55 (see *Charts, page 23*). Only **odd numbered** rows are charted. Refer to Row 8 for all **even numbered** rows.

Dishcloth

Needles: Cast on 34 sts.

Knook: Ch 34; pick up 33 sts on foundation ch: 34 sts.

Rows 1-7: Knit across.

Row 8 AND ALL WRONG SIDE ROWS THROUGH Row 56: K5, P 24, K5.

Row 9 (Right side)**:** K 13, P3, K 18.

Row 11: K 13, P3, K 18.

Row 13: K7, P4, K2, P3, K2, P4, K1, P4, K7.

Row 15: K7, P4, K2, P3, K2, P4, K1, P4, K7.

Row 17: K7, P4, K2, P3, K2, P4, K1, P4, K7.

Row 19: K7, P4, K2, P3, K2, P4, K1, P4, K7.

Row 21: K7, P4, K2, P3, K2, P4, K1, P4, K7.

Row 23: K7, P4, K2, P3, K2, P4, K1, P4, K7.

Row 25: K 13, P3, K 18.

Row 27: K 13, P3, K 18.

Row 29: K5, P 24, K5.

Row 31: K5, P 24, K5.

Row 33: K 13, P3, K 18.

Row 35: K 12, P3, K 19.

Row 37: K5, P1, K6, P3, K 13
P1, K5.

Row 39: K5, P1, K5, P3, K 14
P1, K5.

Row 41: K5, P2, K4, P3, K 13
P2, K5.

Row 43: K5, P2, K3, P3, K 14
P2, K5.

Row 45: K5, P3, K2, P3, K 13
P3, K5.

Row 47: K5, P3, K1, P3, K 14
P3, K5.

Row 49: K5, P4, K3, P 10, K3
P4, K5.

Row 51: K5, P4, K3, P 10, K3
P4, K5.

Row 53: K5, P 24, K5.

Row 55: K5, P 24, K5.

Rows 57-63: Knit across.

Bind off all sts in **knit**.

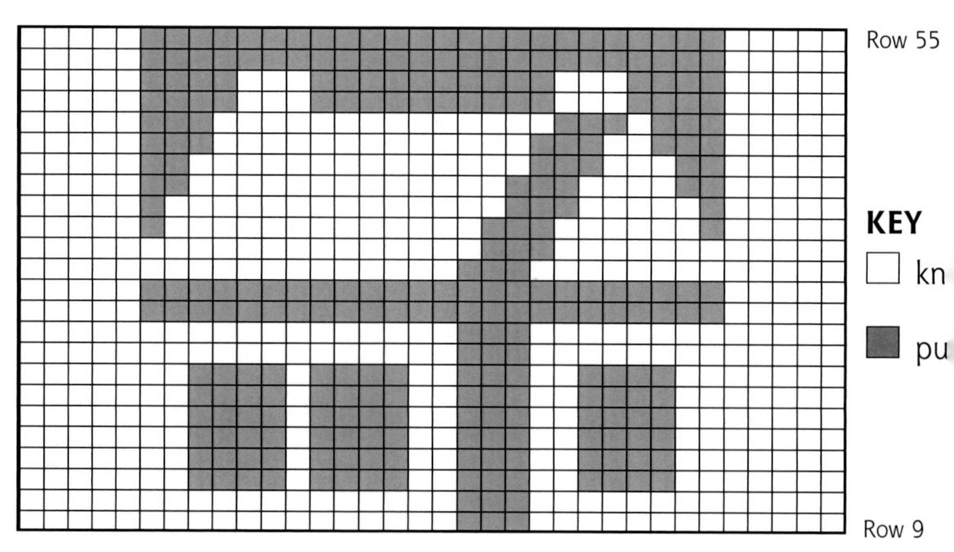

HOOFLY

wn on Back Cover.

ISHED SIZE:
:"w x 9½"h (19 cm x 24 cm)

TERIALS
dium Weight
ton Yarn
2.5 ounces, 120 yards
71 grams, 109 meters) per
ball]: One ball
edles: Straight knitting
needles, size 8 (5 mm) **or**
size needed for gauge
ook: Size H (5 mm) **or**
size needed for gauge

UGE:
Stockinette Stitch
it one row, purl one row),
ts and 13 rows = 2" (5 cm)

ne **dishcloth** may be made
y following the written
structions or by following
ne chart for Rows 9-55
ee *Charts, page 23*). Only
dd numbered rows are
narted. Refer to Row 8 for
l even numbered rows.

ishcloth

edles: Cast on 34 sts.

ook: Ch 34; pick up 33 sts on
undation ch: 34 sts.

ows 1-7: Knit across.

**ow 8 AND ALL WRONG SIDE
OWS THROUGH Row 56:** K5,
24, K5.

Row 9 (Right side)**:** K 12, P1, K8, P1, K 12.

Row 11: K 11, P2, K8, P2, K 11.

Row 13: K 10, P3, K8, P3, K 10.

Row 15: K9, P4, K8, P4, K9.

Row 17: K8, (P5, K8) twice.

Row 19: K7, P6, K8, P6, K7.

Row 21: K6, P7, K8, P7, K6.

Row 23: K5, P8, K8, P8, K5.

Row 25: K 13, P8, K 13.

Row 27: K 13, P8, K 13.

Row 29: K 13, P8, K 13.

Row 31: K 13, P8, K 13.

Row 33: K 13, P8, K 13.

Row 35: K 13, P8, K 13.

Row 37: K 13, P8, K 13.

Row 39: K 13, P8, K 13.

Row 41: K5, P8, K8, P8, K5.

Row 43: K6, P7, K8, P7, K6.

Row 45: K7, P6, K8, P6, K7.

Row 47: K8, (P5, K8) twice.

Row 49: K9, P4, K8, P4, K9.

Row 51: K 10, P3, K8, P3, K 10.

Row 53: K 11, P2, K8, P2, K 11.

Row 55: K 12, P1, K8, P1, K 12.

Rows 57-63: Knit across.

Bind off all sts in **knit**.

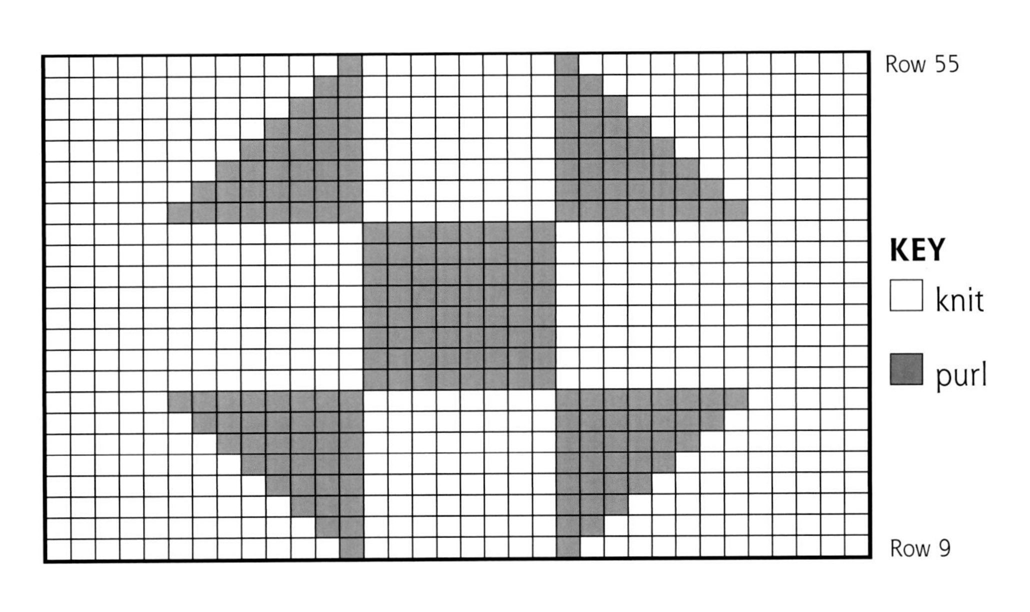

SPLIT NINE PATCH

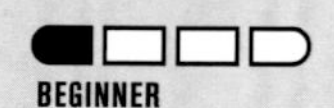

Shown on Back Cover.

FINISHED SIZE:
$7^1/_2$"w x $9^1/_2$"h (19 cm x 24 cm)

MATERIALS
Medium Weight Cotton Yarn (MEDIUM 4)
[2.5 ounces, 120 yards (71 grams, 109 meters) per ball]: One ball
Needles: Straight knitting needles, size 8 (5 mm) **or** size needed for gauge
Knook: Size H (5mm) **or** size needed for gauge

GAUGE:
In Stockinette Stitch
(knit one row, purl one row),
9 sts and 13 rows = 2" (5 cm)

The **dishcloth** may be made by following the written instructions or by following the chart for Rows 9-55 (see *Charts, page 23*). Only **odd numbered** rows are charted. Refer to Row 8 for all **even numbered** rows.

Dishcloth

Needles: Cast on 34 sts.

Knook: Ch 34; pick up 33 sts on foundation ch: 34 sts.

Rows 1-7: Knit across.

Row 8 AND ALL WRONG SIDE ROWS THROUGH Row 56: K5, P 24, K5.

Row 9 (Right side)**:** K 12, P9, K 13.

Row 11: K 11, P2, K1, P7, K 13.

Row 13: K 10, P3, K2, P6, K 13.

Row 15: K9, P4, K3, P5, K 13.

Row 17: K8, P5, K4, P4, K 13.

Row 19: K7, P6, K5, P3, K 13.

Row 21: K6, P7, K6, P2, K 13.

Row 23: K5, P8, K7, P1, K 13.

Row 25: K5, P1, K7, P 16, K5.

Row 27: K5, P2, K6, P8, K1, P7, K5.

Row 29: K5, P3, K5, P8, K2, P6, K5.

Row 31: K5, P4, K4, P8, K3, P5, K5.

Row 33: K5, P5, K3, P8, K4, P4, K5.

Row 35: K5, P6, K2, P8, K5, K5.

Row 37: K5, P7, K1, P8, K6, K5.

Row 39: K5, P 16, K7, P1, K5

Row 41: K 13, P1, K7, P8, K5

Row 43: K 13, P2, K6, P7, K6

Row 45: K 13, P3, K5, P6, K7

Row 47: K 13, P4, K4, P5, K8

Row 49: K 13, P5, K3, P4, K9

Row 51: K 13, P6, K2, P3, K

Row 53: K 13, P7, K1, P2, K

Row 55: K 13, P9, K 12.

Rows 57-63: Knit across.

Bind off all sts in **knit**.

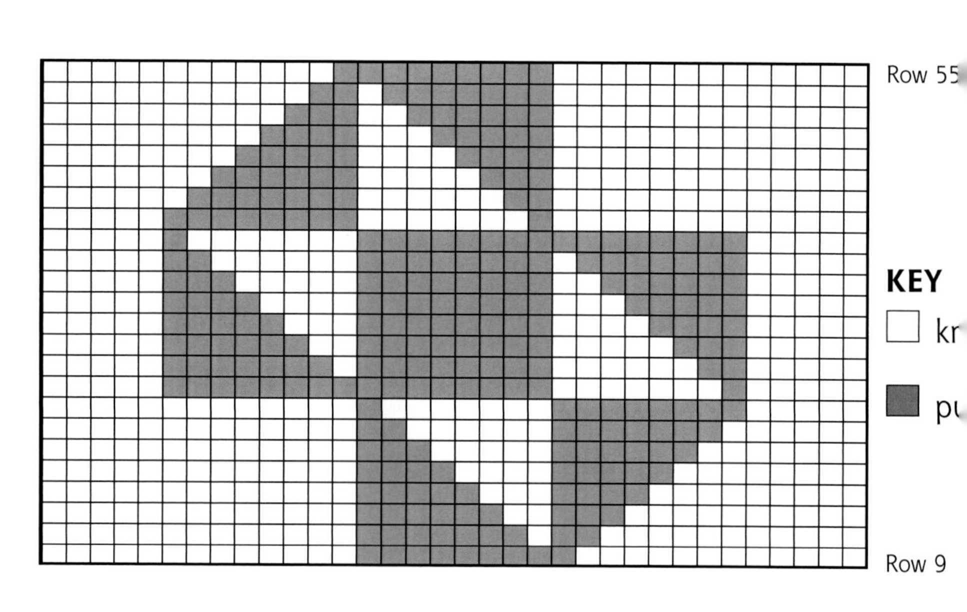

NNIE'S CHOICE

wn on Back Cover.

ISHED SIZE:
"w x 9½"h (19 cm x 24 cm)

ATERIALS
dium Weight
ton Yarn
1.75 ounces, 80 yards
50 grams, 73 meters) per
ball]: One ball
edles: Straight knitting
needles, size 8 (5 mm) **or**
size needed for gauge
ook: Size H (5 mm) **or**
size needed for gauge

UGE:
Stockinette Stitch
it one row, purl one row),
ts and 13 rows = 2" (5 cm)

ne **dishcloth** may be made
y following the written
structions or by following
ne chart for Rows 9-55
ee *Charts, page 23*). Only
dd numbered rows are
harted. Refer to Row 8 for
l **even numbered** rows.

ishcloth

eedles: Cast on 34 sts.

ook: Ch 34; pick up 33 sts on
undation ch: 34 sts.

ows 1-7: Knit across.

ow 8 AND ALL WRONG SIDE OWS THROUGH Row 56: K5, 24, K5.

ow 9 (Right side)**:** K5, P 12, , (P1, K5) twice.

Row 11: K6, P5, K1, P5, (K4, P2) twice, K5.

Row 13: K7, P4, K2, P4, (K3, P3) twice, K5.

Row 15: K8, P3, K3, P3, (K2, P4) twice, K5.

Row 17: K9, P2, K4, P2, (K1, P5) twice, K5.

Row 19: K 10, P1, K5, P 13, K5.

Row 21: K5, P7, K5, P6, K5, P1, K5.

Row 23: K6, P7, K4, P5, K5, P2, K5.

Row 25: K7, P7, K3, P4, K5, P3, K5.

Row 27: K8, P7, K2, P3, K5, P4, K5.

Row 29: K9, P7, K1, P2, K5, P5, K5.

Row 31: K 10, P8, K5, P6, K5.

Row 33: K5, P6, K5, P8, K 10.

Row 35: K5, P5, K5, P2, K1, P7, K9.

Row 37: K5, P4, K5, P3, K2, P7, K8.

Row 39: K5, P3, K5, P4, K3, P7, K7.

Row 41: K5, P2, K5, P5, K4, P7, K6.

Row 43: K5, P1, K5, P6, K5, P7, K5.

Row 45: K5, P 13, K5, P1, K 10.

Row 47: K5, (P5, K1) twice, P2, K4, P2, K9.

Row 49: K5, (P4, K2) twice, P3, K3, P3, K8.

Row 51: K5, (P3, K3) twice, P4, K2, P4, K7.

Row 53: K5, (P2, K4) twice, P5, K1, P5, K6.

Row 55: K5, (P1, K5) twice, P 12, K5.

Rows 57-63: Knit across.

Bind off all sts in **knit**.

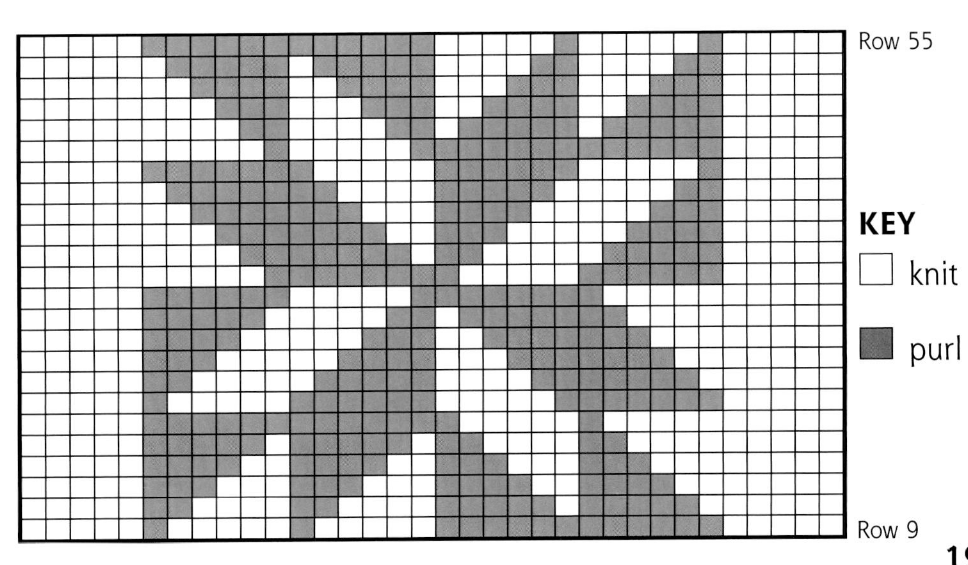

FAR MORE THAN JUST DISHCLOTHS

These wonderful blocks can be stitched together to create a cozy afghan!

Ball

ABBREVIATIONS

ch	chain
cm	centimeters
K	knit
mm	millimeters
P	purl
st(s)	stitch(es)

( ) or **[ ]** - work enclosed instructions **as many** times as specified by the number immediately following **or** contains explanatory remarks.
colon (:) - the number given after a colon at the end of a row denotes the number of stitches on that row.

GAUGE

The gauge and finished size given are for your convenience and are meant only as a guide. Gauge is not of great importance; your **dishcloth** can certainly be a little larger or smaller, without changing the overall effect.

Yarn Weight Symbol & Names	LACE 0	SUPER FINE 1	FINE 2	LIGHT 3	MEDIUM 4	BULKY 5	SUPER BULKY 6
Type of Yarns in Category	Fingering, size 10 crochet thread	Sock, Fingering, Baby	Sport, Baby	DK, Light Worsted	Worsted, Afghan, Aran	Chunky, Craft, Rug	Bulky, Roving
Knit Gauge Range* in Stockinette St to 4" (10 cm)	33-40** sts	27-32 sts	23-26 sts	21-24 sts	16-20 sts	12-15 sts	6-11 sts
Advised Needle Size Range	000-1	1 to 3	3 to 5	5 to 7	7 to 9	9 to 11	11 and larger

*GUIDELINES ONLY: The chart above reflects the most commonly used gauges and needle sizes for specific yarn categories.

** Lace weight yarns are usually knitted on larger needles to create lacy openwork patterns. Accordingly, a gauge range is difficult to determine. Always follow the gauge stated in your pattern.

For complete instructions on how to Knook and vi support, visit www.leisurearts.com.

KNIT STITCH *(abbreviated K)*

With the yarn in **back** of the needles, insert the right needle into the first stitch on the left needle from **left** to **right**. Bring the yarn **between** the needles from **left** to **right** (***Fig. 1a***). Bring the right needle with the loop of yarn toward you an through the stitch (***Fig. 1b***), slipping the worked stitch off the left needle.

Fig. 1a

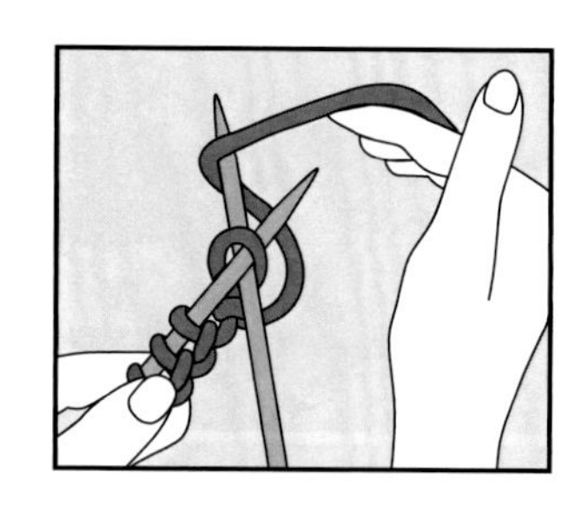

Fig. 1b

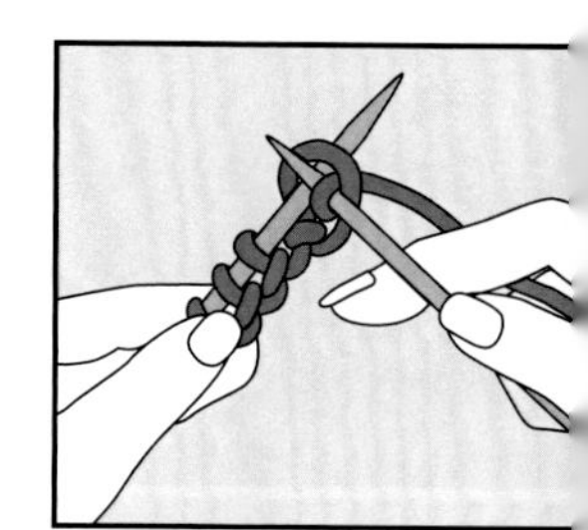

KNIT TERMINOLOGY	
UNITED STATES	**INTERNATIONAL**
gauge =	tension
bind off =	cast off
yarn over (YO) =	yarn forward (yfwd) **or** yarn around needle (yrn)

KNITTING NEEDLES																
U.S.	0	1	2	3	4	5	6	7	8	9	10	10½	11	13	15	17
U.K.	13	12	11	10	9	8	7	6	5	4	3	2	1	00	000	---
Metric - mm	2	2.25	2.75	3.25	3.5	3.75	4	4.5	5	5.5	6	6.5	8	9	10	12.75

BEGINNER	Projects for first-time knitters using basic knit and purl stitches. Minimal shaping.
EASY	Projects using basic stitches, repetitive stitch patterns, simple color changes, and simple shaping and finishing.
INTERMEDIATE	Projects with a variety of stitches, such as basic cables and lace, simple intarsia, double-pointed needles and knitting in the round needle techniques, mid-level shaping and finishing.
EXPERIENCED	Projects using advanced techniques and stitches, such as short rows, fair isle, more intricate intarsia, cables, lace patterns, and numerous color changes.

IRL STITCH (*abbreviated P*)

h the yarn in **front** of the needles, insert the ıt needle into the first stitch on the left needle n **right** to **left**. Bring the yarn **over** the right ·dle to the back, then forward **under** it *j. 2a)*. Bring the right needle with the loop of n away from you and through the stitch *j. 2b)*, slipping the worked stitch off the left ·dle.

. 2a

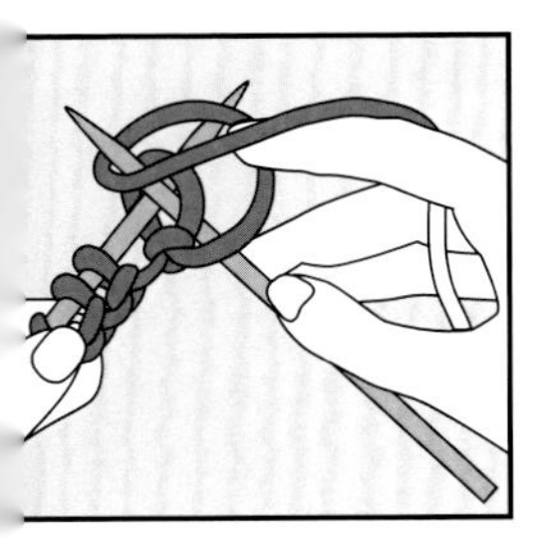

Fig. 2b

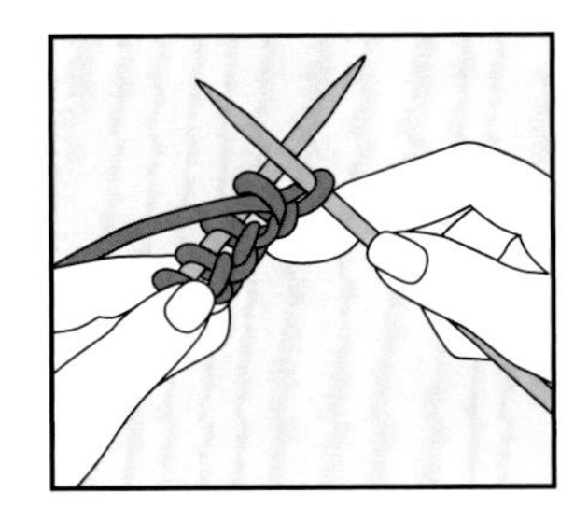

ARTS

ı might find following a chart easier than lowing written instructions, as you can see what ː pattern looks like and you can also see each v at a glance. If you've never knitted from a chart fore, you can refer to the chart while you read the itten instructions until you are comfortable with ː process.

.ualize the chart as your fabric, beginning at the ttom edge and looking at the right side. The chart ɔws each stitch as a square.

.ly **right** side rows are charted; follow the chart m **right** to **left**. Knit the white squares and purl ː shaded squares.

r ease in following the chart, place a ruler on the art above the row being worked to help you keep ur place.

BINDING OFF

Knit the first two stitches. Insert the left needle into the second stitch on the right needle. Lift the second stitch up over the first stitch (***Fig. 3a***) and off the right needle (***Fig. 3b***). Repeat this process until there is only one stitch on the right needle. Cut the yarn, slip the stitch off the right needle, pull the end through the stitch and tighten to secure (***Fig. 3c***).

Fig. 3a

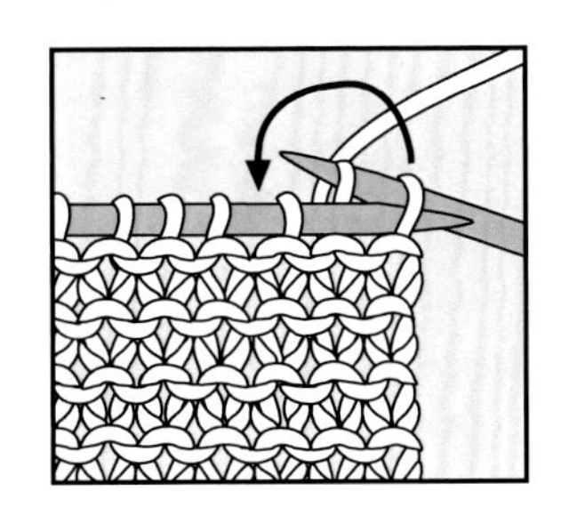

Fig. 3b

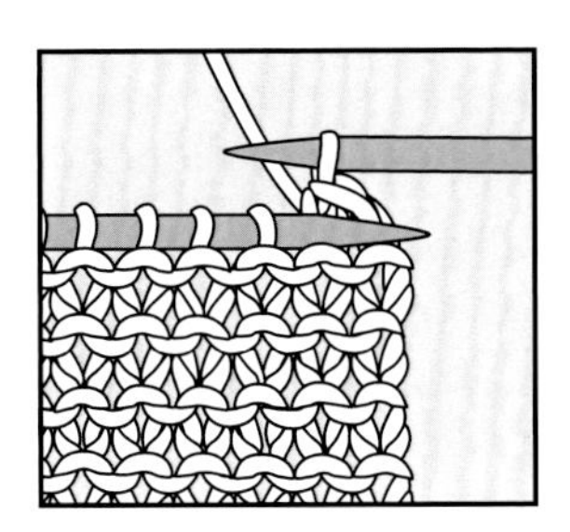

Fig. 3c

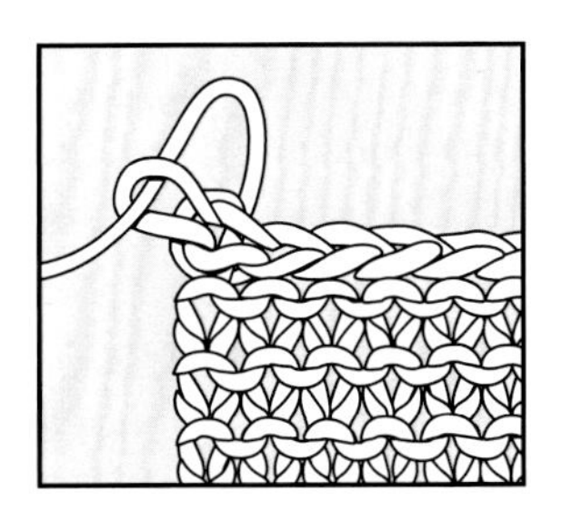

YARN INFORMATION

Each **Dishcloth** in this leaflet was made using medium weight cotton yarn. Any brand of medium weigh cotton yarn may be used. It is best to refer to the yardage/meters when determining how many balls or skeins to purchase. Remember, to arrive at the finished size, it is the GAUGE/TENSION that is important, the brand of yarn. For your convenience, listed below are the specific yarns used to create our photogra models.

AMISH DIAMOND
Lily® Sugar 'n Cream®
#18083 Cornflower Blue

VARIABLE STAR
Lily® Sugar 'n Cream®
#00001 White

PINWHEEL
Lily® Sugar 'n Cream®
#01612 Country Yellow

ARROW POINT
Lily® Sugar 'n Cream®
#18712 Hot Green

KING'S CROWN
Lily® Sugar 'n Cream®
#01740 Hot Pink

BACHELOR'S PUZZLE
Lily® Sugar 'n Cream®
#00001 White

OLD MAID'S PUZZLE
Bernat® Handicrafter® Cotton
#13699 Tangerine

DUTCHMAN'S PUZZLE
Lily® Sugar 'n Cream®
#01612 Country Yellow

NINE PATCH
Lily® Sugar 'n Cream®
#18712 Hot Green

FRIENDSHIP STAR
Lily® Sugar 'n Cream®
#01740 Hot Pink

WINDBLOWN SQUARE
Lily® Sugar 'n Cream®
#00009 Bright Navy

HOUSE
Lily® Sugar 'n Cream®
#18083 Cornflower Blue

SHOOFLY
Lily® Sugar 'n Cream®
#00095 Red

SPLIT NINE PATCH
Lily® Sugar 'n Cream®
#00009 Bright Navy

ANNIE'S CHOICE
Bernat® Handicrafter® Cottor
#13699 Tangerine

We have made every effort to ensure that these instructions are accurate and complete.
We cannot, however, be responsible for human error, typographical mistakes, or variations in individual work.

PRODUCTION TEAM

Technical Writer/Editor: Linda A. Daley
Editorial Writer: Susan McManus Johnson
Photography Manager: Katherine Laughlin
Photo Stylist: Christy Meyers
Photographer: Mark Mathews
Graphic Design & Layout: Shibaguyz Designz, Jason Mullett-Bowlsby, Manager